Funny
Fish

Cynthia Rider • Alex Brychta

OXFORD
UNIVERSITY PRESS

Mum   Dad   Biff

Chip   Kipper   Floppy

Kipper was fishing.

He got a hat.

Biff was fishing.

She got a crab.

Chip was fishing.

He got an octopus!

Mum was fishing.

She got a bucket.

Dad was fishing.

He got a boot.

SPLASH!

Floppy got a fish!

Think about the story

Why do you think Floppy fell into the water?

Who do you think caught the funniest fish?

What would you do if you caught a big crab, like Biff?

Floppy's fish lives in the sea. Where else do fish live?

Tangled lines

Follow the lines to see who gets the fish.